45 Salmon Recipes for Home

By: Kelly Johnson

Table of Contents

- Classic Baked Salmon
- Grilled Lemon Dill Salmon
- Honey Mustard Glazed Salmon
- Teriyaki Salmon Skewers
- Baked Maple Soy Salmon
- Garlic Parmesan Crusted Salmon
- Citrus Herb Grilled Salmon
- Blackened Cajun Salmon
- Pesto Crusted Salmon
- Orange Glazed Salmon
- Balsamic Glazed Salmon
- Thai Coconut Curry Salmon
- Sesame Ginger Glazed Salmon
- Lemon Herb Butter Baked Salmon
- Mediterranean Herb Crusted Salmon
- Smoked Salmon Platter
- Pineapple Mango Salsa Salmon
- Almond Crusted Salmon
- Cilantro Lime Grilled Salmon
- Dijon Herb Crusted Salmon
- Harissa Spiced Salmon
- Maple Pecan Crusted Salmon
- Spicy Sriracha Glazed Salmon
- Lemon Garlic Butter Poached Salmon
- Honey Walnut Crusted Salmon
- Mediterranean Salmon Salad
- Wasabi Sesame Crusted Salmon
- Chimichurri Grilled Salmon
- Raspberry Balsamic Glazed Salmon
- Tequila Lime Grilled Salmon
- Pistachio Crusted Salmon
- Mango Avocado Salmon Tartare
- Jerk Spiced Grilled Salmon
- Caprese Stuffed Salmon
- Lemon Dill Salmon Burgers

- Soy Ginger Glazed Salmon
- Sweet Chili Lime Baked Salmon
- Salmon with Creamy Lemon Dill Sauce
- Spinach and Feta Stuffed Salmon
- Garlic Butter Tuscan Salmon
- Lemon Herb Quinoa with Salmon
- Coconut Lime Salmon Skewers
- Walnut Pesto Salmon
- Cajun Salmon Alfredo Pasta
- Baked Salmon with Herbed Yogurt Sauce

Classic Baked Salmon

Ingredients:

- 4 salmon fillets
- 2 tablespoons olive oil
- 2 tablespoons fresh lemon juice
- 2 cloves garlic, minced
- 1 teaspoon dried oregano
- 1 teaspoon dried thyme
- Salt and black pepper, to taste
- Lemon wedges (for serving)
- Fresh parsley, chopped (for garnish)

Instructions:

Preheat the oven to 400°F (200°C).
Place the salmon fillets on a baking sheet lined with parchment paper or lightly greased.
In a small bowl, whisk together olive oil, lemon juice, minced garlic, dried oregano, dried thyme, salt, and black pepper.
Brush the olive oil and lemon mixture over the salmon fillets, ensuring they are well-coated.
Bake in the preheated oven for 12-15 minutes or until the salmon flakes easily with a fork. Cooking time may vary based on the thickness of the fillets.
If desired, broil for an additional 2-3 minutes to give the salmon a golden crust.
Remove from the oven and let it rest for a few minutes.
Serve the Classic Baked Salmon with lemon wedges and a sprinkle of chopped fresh parsley.
Enjoy this simple and delicious baked salmon as a nutritious main dish!

Grilled Lemon Dill Salmon

Ingredients:

- 4 salmon fillets
- 2 tablespoons olive oil
- Zest of 1 lemon
- Juice of 1 lemon
- 3 tablespoons fresh dill, chopped
- 2 cloves garlic, minced
- Salt and black pepper, to taste
- Lemon wedges (for serving)

Instructions:

Preheat the grill to medium-high heat.
In a bowl, combine olive oil, lemon zest, lemon juice, chopped dill, minced garlic, salt, and black pepper. Mix well to create the marinade.
Place the salmon fillets in a shallow dish and brush them with the marinade, ensuring both sides are well-coated. Let it marinate for at least 15-30 minutes.
Grease the grill grates to prevent sticking. Place the marinated salmon fillets on the preheated grill.
Grill the salmon for 4-6 minutes per side, depending on thickness, or until it easily flakes with a fork. Baste the fillets with the remaining marinade during grilling.
Remove the salmon from the grill and let it rest for a few minutes.
Serve the Grilled Lemon Dill Salmon with additional lemon wedges for squeezing over the top.
Garnish with extra fresh dill if desired.
Enjoy this light and flavorful grilled salmon with the zesty combination of lemon and dill!

Honey Mustard Glazed Salmon

Ingredients:

- 4 salmon fillets
- 1/4 cup Dijon mustard
- 2 tablespoons whole grain mustard
- 2 tablespoons honey
- 2 tablespoons soy sauce
- 2 cloves garlic, minced
- 1 tablespoon olive oil
- Salt and black pepper, to taste
- Fresh parsley, chopped (for garnish)

Instructions:

Preheat the oven to 400°F (200°C).
In a bowl, whisk together Dijon mustard, whole grain mustard, honey, soy sauce, minced garlic, olive oil, salt, and black pepper to create the honey mustard glaze.
Place the salmon fillets on a baking sheet lined with parchment paper or lightly greased.
Brush the honey mustard glaze over the salmon fillets, ensuring they are well-coated.
Bake in the preheated oven for 12-15 minutes or until the salmon flakes easily with a fork. Cooking time may vary based on the thickness of the fillets.
If desired, broil for an additional 2-3 minutes to caramelize the glaze and give the salmon a golden finish.
Remove from the oven and let it rest for a few minutes.
Serve the Honey Mustard Glazed Salmon, drizzled with any remaining glaze and garnished with chopped fresh parsley.
Enjoy this sweet and savory glazed salmon for a delightful and easy-to-make meal!

Teriyaki Salmon Skewers

Ingredients:

- 1 pound salmon fillets, cut into cubes
- 1/4 cup soy sauce
- 2 tablespoons mirin
- 2 tablespoons sake or dry white wine
- 2 tablespoons brown sugar
- 1 tablespoon honey
- 2 cloves garlic, minced
- 1 teaspoon fresh ginger, grated
- Sesame seeds (for garnish)
- Green onions, sliced (for garnish)
- Wooden skewers, soaked in water

Instructions:

In a bowl, whisk together soy sauce, mirin, sake or white wine, brown sugar, honey, minced garlic, and grated ginger to create the teriyaki marinade.
Cut the salmon fillets into bite-sized cubes.
Place the salmon cubes in a shallow dish and pour the teriyaki marinade over them. Ensure all pieces are well-coated. Let it marinate in the refrigerator for at least 30 minutes.
Preheat the grill or grill pan to medium-high heat.
Thread the marinated salmon cubes onto the soaked wooden skewers.
Grill the salmon skewers for about 3-4 minutes per side or until the salmon is cooked through and has a nice grill marks.
Brush the skewers with any remaining teriyaki marinade during grilling.
Once cooked, remove the skewers from the grill.
Sprinkle sesame seeds and sliced green onions over the Teriyaki Salmon Skewers for garnish.
Serve immediately over rice or with your favorite side dishes.
Enjoy these flavorful and tender teriyaki salmon skewers for a delicious and satisfying meal!

Baked Maple Soy Salmon

Ingredients:

- 4 salmon fillets
- 1/4 cup soy sauce
- 2 tablespoons maple syrup
- 2 tablespoons olive oil
- 2 cloves garlic, minced
- 1 teaspoon Dijon mustard
- 1 teaspoon fresh ginger, grated
- Salt and black pepper, to taste
- Sesame seeds (for garnish)
- Green onions, sliced (for garnish)

Instructions:

Preheat the oven to 400°F (200°C).
In a bowl, whisk together soy sauce, maple syrup, olive oil, minced garlic, Dijon mustard, grated ginger, salt, and black pepper to create the maple soy marinade.
Place the salmon fillets in a baking dish or on a baking sheet lined with parchment paper.
Pour the maple soy marinade over the salmon fillets, ensuring they are well-coated. Let them marinate for about 15-30 minutes.
Bake in the preheated oven for 12-15 minutes or until the salmon flakes easily with a fork. Cooking time may vary based on the thickness of the fillets.
If desired, broil for an additional 2-3 minutes to caramelize the glaze.
Remove from the oven and let it rest for a few minutes.
Sprinkle sesame seeds and sliced green onions over the Baked Maple Soy Salmon for garnish.
Serve the salmon over rice or with your favorite side dishes.
Enjoy this sweet and savory baked maple soy salmon for a delightful and easy-to-make meal!

Garlic Parmesan Crusted Salmon

Ingredients:

- 4 salmon fillets
- 1/2 cup grated Parmesan cheese
- 1/4 cup breadcrumbs
- 2 tablespoons melted butter
- 2 tablespoons fresh parsley, chopped
- 2 cloves garlic, minced
- 1 teaspoon lemon zest
- Salt and black pepper, to taste
- Lemon wedges (for serving)

Instructions:

Preheat the oven to 400°F (200°C).
In a bowl, combine grated Parmesan cheese, breadcrumbs, melted butter, chopped fresh parsley, minced garlic, lemon zest, salt, and black pepper. Mix well to create the crust mixture.
Place the salmon fillets on a baking sheet lined with parchment paper.
Press the Parmesan mixture onto the top of each salmon fillet, ensuring an even coating.
Bake in the preheated oven for 12-15 minutes or until the salmon is cooked through and the crust is golden brown. Cooking time may vary based on the thickness of the fillets.
If desired, broil for an additional 2-3 minutes to achieve a crispier crust.
Remove from the oven and let it rest for a few minutes.
Serve the Garlic Parmesan Crusted Salmon with lemon wedges on the side.
Enjoy this flavorful and cheesy crusted salmon for a delicious and elegant meal!

Citrus Herb Grilled Salmon

Ingredients:

- 4 salmon fillets
- 1/4 cup olive oil
- 2 tablespoons fresh lemon juice
- 2 tablespoons fresh orange juice
- 2 cloves garlic, minced
- 1 tablespoon fresh parsley, chopped
- 1 tablespoon fresh dill, chopped
- 1 teaspoon lemon zest
- Salt and black pepper, to taste
- Lemon wedges (for serving)

Instructions:

In a bowl, whisk together olive oil, fresh lemon juice, fresh orange juice, minced garlic, chopped fresh parsley, chopped fresh dill, lemon zest, salt, and black pepper to create the citrus herb marinade.

Place the salmon fillets in a shallow dish and pour the marinade over them. Ensure the fillets are well-coated. Let them marinate in the refrigerator for at least 30 minutes.

Preheat the grill to medium-high heat.

Remove the salmon fillets from the marinade and let any excess drip off.

Grill the salmon fillets for about 3-4 minutes per side or until they are cooked through and have distinct grill marks.

Remove from the grill and let it rest for a few minutes.

Serve the Citrus Herb Grilled Salmon with lemon wedges on the side.

Enjoy this light and refreshing grilled salmon with the zesty flavors of citrus and herbs!

Blackened Cajun Salmon

Ingredients:

- 4 salmon fillets
- 2 tablespoons Cajun seasoning
- 1 tablespoon paprika
- 1 teaspoon onion powder
- 1 teaspoon garlic powder
- 1 teaspoon thyme, dried
- 1 teaspoon oregano, dried
- 1/2 teaspoon cayenne pepper (adjust to taste)
- Salt and black pepper, to taste
- 2 tablespoons olive oil
- Lemon wedges (for serving)

Instructions:

In a small bowl, mix together Cajun seasoning, paprika, onion powder, garlic powder, thyme, oregano, cayenne pepper, salt, and black pepper to create the blackened Cajun spice rub.

Pat the salmon fillets dry with paper towels.

Rub the blackened Cajun spice mix generously over each side of the salmon fillets.

Heat olive oil in a skillet or cast-iron pan over medium-high heat.

Place the seasoned salmon fillets in the hot skillet and cook for about 3-4 minutes per side or until the salmon is cooked through and has a blackened crust. Cooking time may vary based on the thickness of the fillets.

Remove from the skillet and let the salmon rest for a few minutes.

Serve the Blackened Cajun Salmon with lemon wedges on the side.

Enjoy this flavorful and spicy Cajun-inspired salmon for a delicious and bold meal! Adjust the cayenne pepper according to your spice preference.

Pesto Crusted Salmon

Ingredients:

- 4 salmon fillets
- 1/2 cup fresh basil leaves, packed
- 1/4 cup pine nuts
- 1/4 cup grated Parmesan cheese
- 2 cloves garlic, minced
- 1/3 cup extra-virgin olive oil
- Salt and black pepper, to taste
- Lemon wedges (for serving)

Instructions:

Preheat the oven to 400°F (200°C).
In a food processor, combine fresh basil leaves, pine nuts, grated Parmesan cheese, minced garlic, and a pinch of salt. Pulse until finely chopped.
With the food processor running, gradually add the olive oil until the mixture forms a smooth pesto.
Place the salmon fillets on a baking sheet lined with parchment paper.
Spread a generous layer of pesto over the top of each salmon fillet.
Bake in the preheated oven for 12-15 minutes or until the salmon is cooked through and the pesto crust is golden brown. Cooking time may vary based on the thickness of the fillets.
Remove from the oven and let it rest for a few minutes.
Serve the Pesto Crusted Salmon with lemon wedges on the side.
Enjoy this delicious and herby pesto-crusted salmon for a vibrant and flavorful meal!

Orange Glazed Salmon

Ingredients:

- 4 salmon fillets
- 1/2 cup orange juice
- 1/4 cup soy sauce
- 2 tablespoons honey
- 1 tablespoon Dijon mustard
- 2 cloves garlic, minced
- 1 teaspoon grated fresh ginger
- 1 tablespoon olive oil
- Sesame seeds (for garnish, optional)
- Green onions, sliced (for garnish, optional)
- Orange slices (for garnish, optional)

Instructions:

In a bowl, whisk together orange juice, soy sauce, honey, Dijon mustard, minced garlic, and grated fresh ginger to create the orange glaze.
Pat the salmon fillets dry with paper towels.
Heat olive oil in a skillet over medium-high heat.
Place the salmon fillets in the hot skillet and cook for about 3-4 minutes per side or until they are browned and cooked through.
Pour the orange glaze over the salmon fillets in the skillet. Allow the glaze to simmer and coat the salmon for an additional 1-2 minutes.
Remove from the skillet and let the salmon rest for a few minutes.
Garnish with sesame seeds, sliced green onions, and orange slices if desired.
Serve the Orange Glazed Salmon over rice or with your favorite side dish.
Enjoy this sweet and tangy orange-glazed salmon for a burst of citrusy flavor!

Balsamic Glazed Salmon

Ingredients:

- 4 salmon fillets
- 1/4 cup balsamic vinegar
- 2 tablespoons honey
- 2 tablespoons soy sauce
- 2 cloves garlic, minced
- 1 teaspoon Dijon mustard
- 1 tablespoon olive oil
- Salt and black pepper, to taste
- Fresh parsley, chopped (for garnish, optional)

Instructions:

In a small bowl, whisk together balsamic vinegar, honey, soy sauce, minced garlic, and Dijon mustard to create the balsamic glaze.

Pat the salmon fillets dry with paper towels.

Heat olive oil in a skillet over medium-high heat.

Place the salmon fillets in the hot skillet and cook for about 3-4 minutes per side or until they are browned and cooked through.

Pour the balsamic glaze over the salmon fillets in the skillet. Allow the glaze to simmer and coat the salmon for an additional 1-2 minutes.

Season with salt and black pepper to taste.

Remove from the skillet and let the salmon rest for a few minutes.

Garnish with chopped fresh parsley if desired.

Serve the Balsamic Glazed Salmon over quinoa, rice, or with your favorite side.

Enjoy this flavorful and tangy balsamic-glazed salmon for a delightful meal!

Thai Coconut Curry Salmon

Ingredients:

- 4 salmon fillets
- 1 can (14 oz) coconut milk
- 2 tablespoons red curry paste
- 2 tablespoons fish sauce
- 1 tablespoon brown sugar
- 1 tablespoon lime juice
- 2 tablespoons vegetable oil
- 1 red bell pepper, thinly sliced
- 1 zucchini, thinly sliced
- 1 carrot, julienned
- 2 cloves garlic, minced
- Fresh cilantro, chopped (for garnish, optional)
- Cooked jasmine rice (for serving)

Instructions:

In a bowl, whisk together coconut milk, red curry paste, fish sauce, brown sugar, and lime juice to create the curry sauce. Set aside.
Heat vegetable oil in a large skillet over medium-high heat.
Add minced garlic and sauté for about 1 minute until fragrant.
Add sliced red bell pepper, zucchini, and julienned carrot to the skillet. Cook for 2-3 minutes until the vegetables are slightly tender.
Push the vegetables to the side and place the salmon fillets in the skillet. Cook for 2-3 minutes per side or until the salmon is browned.
Pour the curry sauce over the salmon and vegetables. Simmer for an additional 5-7 minutes, allowing the flavors to meld and the salmon to cook through.
Season with salt and pepper to taste.
Remove from heat and garnish with fresh cilantro if desired.
Serve the Thai Coconut Curry Salmon over cooked jasmine rice.
Enjoy this aromatic and creamy Thai coconut curry salmon for a delicious and satisfying meal!

Sesame Ginger Glazed Salmon

Ingredients:

- 4 salmon fillets
- 1/4 cup soy sauce
- 2 tablespoons honey
- 1 tablespoon sesame oil
- 1 tablespoon rice vinegar
- 1 tablespoon fresh ginger, grated
- 2 cloves garlic, minced
- 1 tablespoon sesame seeds (for garnish, optional)
- Green onions, sliced (for garnish, optional)

Instructions:

Preheat the oven to 400°F (200°C).
In a bowl, whisk together soy sauce, honey, sesame oil, rice vinegar, grated ginger, and minced garlic to create the glaze.
Place the salmon fillets on a baking sheet lined with parchment paper.
Brush the glaze over each salmon fillet, ensuring they are well coated.
Bake in the preheated oven for 12-15 minutes or until the salmon is cooked through and flakes easily with a fork.
Optional: Sprinkle sesame seeds and sliced green onions over the glazed salmon for garnish.
Remove from the oven and let it rest for a few minutes.
Serve the Sesame Ginger Glazed Salmon over steamed rice or your favorite side dish.
Enjoy this flavorful and zesty sesame ginger glazed salmon for a delightful meal!

Lemon Herb Butter Baked Salmon

Ingredients:

- 4 salmon fillets
- 1/4 cup unsalted butter, melted
- 2 tablespoons fresh lemon juice
- Zest of one lemon
- 2 cloves garlic, minced
- 1 tablespoon fresh parsley, chopped
- 1 tablespoon fresh dill, chopped
- Salt and black pepper, to taste
- Lemon slices (for garnish, optional)

Instructions:

Preheat the oven to 400°F (200°C).
In a bowl, mix together melted butter, fresh lemon juice, lemon zest, minced garlic, chopped parsley, and chopped dill to create the herb butter mixture.
Place the salmon fillets on a baking sheet lined with parchment paper.
Brush the herb butter mixture over each salmon fillet, ensuring they are well coated.
Season with salt and black pepper to taste.
Optional: Place lemon slices on top of each salmon fillet for additional flavor and presentation.
Bake in the preheated oven for 12-15 minutes or until the salmon is cooked through and flakes easily with a fork.
Remove from the oven and let it rest for a few minutes.
Serve the Lemon Herb Butter Baked Salmon over quinoa, rice, or with your favorite side.
Enjoy this light and aromatic lemon herb butter baked salmon for a delicious and wholesome meal!

Mediterranean Herb Crusted Salmon

Ingredients:

- 4 salmon fillets
- 1/4 cup breadcrumbs (preferably panko)
- 2 tablespoons fresh parsley, chopped
- 1 tablespoon fresh basil, chopped
- 1 tablespoon fresh oregano, chopped
- 2 cloves garlic, minced
- Zest of one lemon
- 2 tablespoons olive oil
- Salt and black pepper, to taste
- Lemon wedges (for serving, optional)

Instructions:

Preheat the oven to 400°F (200°C).
In a bowl, combine breadcrumbs, chopped parsley, chopped basil, chopped oregano, minced garlic, and lemon zest to create the herb crust mixture.
Place the salmon fillets on a baking sheet lined with parchment paper.
Drizzle olive oil over each salmon fillet.
Press the herb crust mixture onto the top of each salmon fillet, ensuring they are evenly coated.
Season with salt and black pepper to taste.
Bake in the preheated oven for 12-15 minutes or until the salmon is cooked through and the crust is golden brown.
Optional: Serve with lemon wedges for a burst of citrus flavor.
Remove from the oven and let it rest for a few minutes.
Serve the Mediterranean Herb-Crusted Salmon over a bed of couscous, quinoa, or your favorite side.
Enjoy this flavorful and herby Mediterranean herb-crusted salmon for a delightful meal!

Smoked Salmon Platter

Ingredients:

- 8 oz smoked salmon slices
- 8 oz cream cheese, softened
- 1 tablespoon capers
- 1 small red onion, thinly sliced
- 1 cucumber, thinly sliced
- 1 lemon, thinly sliced
- Fresh dill sprigs (for garnish)
- Crackers or toasted baguette slices (for serving)

Instructions:

Arrange the smoked salmon slices on a serving platter.
In a small bowl, mix the softened cream cheese until smooth.
Dollop the cream cheese onto the platter alongside the smoked salmon.
Scatter capers over the smoked salmon.
Arrange the thinly sliced red onion, cucumber, and lemon slices around the platter.
Garnish with fresh dill sprigs for added flavor and visual appeal.
Serve the smoked salmon platter with crackers or toasted baguette slices.
Enjoy this elegant and classic smoked salmon platter as a delightful appetizer or light meal!

Pineapple Mango Salsa Salmon

Ingredients:

For the Salmon:

- 4 salmon fillets
- 2 tablespoons olive oil
- Salt and black pepper, to taste
- 1 teaspoon smoked paprika
- 1 teaspoon ground cumin
- 1 teaspoon garlic powder

For the Pineapple Mango Salsa:

- 1 cup fresh pineapple, diced
- 1 cup fresh mango, diced
- 1/4 cup red onion, finely chopped
- 1/4 cup fresh cilantro, chopped
- 1 jalapeño, seeds removed and finely chopped
- Juice of 1 lime
- Salt and black pepper, to taste

Instructions:

Preheat the oven to 400°F (200°C).
Place the salmon fillets on a baking sheet lined with parchment paper.
Drizzle olive oil over each salmon fillet.
In a small bowl, mix salt, black pepper, smoked paprika, ground cumin, and garlic powder. Sprinkle the spice mixture evenly over the salmon fillets.
Bake in the preheated oven for 12-15 minutes or until the salmon is cooked through and flakes easily with a fork.
While the salmon is baking, prepare the pineapple mango salsa. In a bowl, combine diced pineapple, diced mango, finely chopped red onion, chopped cilantro, chopped jalapeño, lime juice, salt, and black pepper. Mix well.
Once the salmon is done, remove it from the oven and transfer the fillets to serving plates.
Spoon the pineapple mango salsa over the top of each salmon fillet.
Optional: Garnish with additional cilantro and lime wedges.

Serve the Pineapple Mango Salsa Salmon with your favorite side dishes. Enjoy this vibrant and tropical-flavored salmon dish!

Almond Crusted Salmon

Ingredients:

- 4 salmon fillets
- 1 cup almonds, finely chopped
- 1/4 cup grated Parmesan cheese
- 1 teaspoon dried thyme
- 1 teaspoon garlic powder
- Salt and black pepper, to taste
- 2 tablespoons Dijon mustard
- 2 tablespoons honey
- 1 tablespoon olive oil
- Lemon wedges (for serving)

Instructions:

Preheat the oven to 400°F (200°C).
In a shallow bowl, combine chopped almonds, grated Parmesan cheese, dried thyme, garlic powder, salt, and black pepper.
In a separate bowl, mix Dijon mustard, honey, and olive oil.
Pat the salmon fillets dry with a paper towel.
Brush each salmon fillet with the Dijon mustard mixture, coating both sides.
Press each salmon fillet into the almond mixture, ensuring a thick and even coating on each side.
Place the almond-crusted salmon fillets on a baking sheet lined with parchment paper.
Bake in the preheated oven for 12-15 minutes or until the salmon is cooked through and the crust is golden brown.
Optional: Serve with lemon wedges for a citrusy kick.
Remove from the oven and let it rest for a few minutes.
Serve the Almond-Crusted Salmon over a bed of quinoa, couscous, or your favorite side.
Enjoy this crunchy and flavorful almond-crusted salmon as a delicious and nutritious meal!

Cilantro Lime Grilled Salmon

Ingredients:

- 4 salmon fillets
- 1/4 cup fresh cilantro, chopped
- 2 tablespoons olive oil
- Zest and juice of 2 limes
- 2 cloves garlic, minced
- 1 teaspoon ground cumin
- Salt and black pepper, to taste
- Lime wedges (for serving)

Instructions:

Preheat the grill to medium-high heat.
In a bowl, mix chopped cilantro, olive oil, lime zest, lime juice, minced garlic, ground cumin, salt, and black pepper.
Place the salmon fillets on a plate or shallow dish.
Brush the cilantro lime marinade over both sides of each salmon fillet, ensuring they are well-coated.
Let the salmon marinate for at least 15-30 minutes to absorb the flavors.
Grease the grill grates to prevent sticking.
Place the marinated salmon fillets on the preheated grill.
Grill for 4-6 minutes per side, or until the salmon is cooked to your liking and easily flakes with a fork.
Optional: Serve with additional lime wedges for a burst of citrus flavor.
Remove the grilled salmon from the heat.
Let it rest for a few minutes before serving.
Serve the Cilantro Lime Grilled Salmon with your favorite grilled vegetables or a side salad.
Enjoy this refreshing and zesty grilled salmon for a light and delicious meal!

Dijon Herb Crusted Salmon

Ingredients:

- 4 salmon fillets
- 2 tablespoons Dijon mustard
- 2 tablespoons olive oil
- 1 cup breadcrumbs (preferably Panko)
- 2 tablespoons fresh parsley, finely chopped
- 1 tablespoon fresh dill, chopped
- 1 teaspoon dried thyme
- Salt and black pepper, to taste
- Lemon wedges (for serving)

Instructions:

Preheat the oven to 400°F (200°C).
In a bowl, mix Dijon mustard and olive oil until well combined.
In another bowl, combine breadcrumbs, chopped parsley, chopped dill, dried thyme, salt, and black pepper.
Pat the salmon fillets dry with a paper towel.
Brush each salmon fillet with the Dijon mustard and olive oil mixture, coating both sides.
Press each salmon fillet into the breadcrumb mixture, ensuring a thick and even coating on each side.
Place the herb-crusted salmon fillets on a baking sheet lined with parchment paper.
Bake in the preheated oven for 12-15 minutes or until the salmon is cooked through and the crust is golden brown.
Optional: Serve with lemon wedges for a citrusy kick.
Remove from the oven and let it rest for a few minutes.
Serve the Dijon Herb-Crusted Salmon over a bed of quinoa, couscous, or your favorite side.
Enjoy this flavorful and herb-infused salmon as a delightful and elegant meal!

Harissa Spiced Salmon

Ingredients:

- 4 salmon fillets
- 2 tablespoons harissa paste
- 2 tablespoons olive oil
- 1 tablespoon honey
- 1 teaspoon ground cumin
- 1 teaspoon smoked paprika
- Salt and black pepper, to taste
- Lemon wedges (for serving)
- Fresh cilantro, chopped (for garnish)

Instructions:

Preheat the oven to 400°F (200°C).
In a bowl, whisk together harissa paste, olive oil, honey, ground cumin, smoked paprika, salt, and black pepper.
Pat the salmon fillets dry with a paper towel.
Brush each salmon fillet with the harissa mixture, coating both sides.
Place the harissa-spiced salmon fillets on a baking sheet lined with parchment paper.
Bake in the preheated oven for 12-15 minutes or until the salmon is cooked through and flakes easily with a fork.
Optional: Serve with lemon wedges for a burst of citrus and sprinkle fresh chopped cilantro on top.
Remove from the oven and let it rest for a few minutes.
Serve the Harissa-Spiced Salmon over couscous, rice, or your favorite grain.
Enjoy this bold and flavorful salmon dish that combines the heat of harissa with sweet honey for a deliciously spicy-sweet experience!

Maple Pecan Crusted Salmon

Ingredients:

- 4 salmon fillets
- 1/4 cup maple syrup
- 1/2 cup pecans, finely chopped
- 2 tablespoons Dijon mustard
- 1 tablespoon olive oil
- 1 teaspoon garlic powder
- Salt and black pepper, to taste
- Lemon wedges (for serving)
- Fresh parsley, chopped (for garnish)

Instructions:

Preheat the oven to 400°F (200°C).
In a bowl, mix together maple syrup, finely chopped pecans, Dijon mustard, olive oil, garlic powder, salt, and black pepper.
Pat the salmon fillets dry with a paper towel.
Brush each salmon fillet with the maple pecan mixture, coating both sides.
Place the maple pecan-crusted salmon fillets on a baking sheet lined with parchment paper.
Bake in the preheated oven for 12-15 minutes or until the salmon is cooked through and flakes easily with a fork.
Optional: Serve with lemon wedges for a hint of citrus and sprinkle fresh chopped parsley on top.
Remove from the oven and let it rest for a few minutes.
Serve the Maple Pecan-Crusted Salmon over a bed of wild rice, quinoa, or your favorite side.
Enjoy this delightful combination of sweet maple and crunchy pecans that add a rich and flavorful crust to the salmon!

Spicy Sriracha Glazed Salmon

Ingredients:

- 4 salmon fillets
- 3 tablespoons soy sauce
- 2 tablespoons Sriracha sauce (adjust to taste for spice level)
- 2 tablespoons honey
- 1 tablespoon sesame oil
- 1 tablespoon rice vinegar
- 1 teaspoon grated ginger
- 2 cloves garlic, minced
- Sesame seeds (for garnish)
- Green onions, sliced (for garnish)

Instructions:

Preheat the oven to 400°F (200°C).
In a bowl, whisk together soy sauce, Sriracha sauce, honey, sesame oil, rice vinegar, grated ginger, and minced garlic.
Pat the salmon fillets dry with a paper towel.
Place the salmon fillets in a shallow dish and pour half of the Sriracha glaze over them, ensuring an even coating.
Marinate the salmon for about 15-20 minutes.
Transfer the marinated salmon to a baking sheet lined with parchment paper.
Bake in the preheated oven for 12-15 minutes or until the salmon is cooked through and easily flakes with a fork.
While baking, heat the remaining Sriracha glaze in a small saucepan over medium heat until it thickens slightly.
Once the salmon is done, brush the thickened Sriracha glaze over the top.
Optional: Garnish with sesame seeds and sliced green onions.
Remove from the oven and let it rest for a few minutes.
Serve the Spicy Sriracha-Glazed Salmon over a bed of jasmine rice or your favorite grain.
Enjoy this deliciously spicy and sweet glazed salmon with a kick of Sriracha!

Lemon Garlic Butter Poached Salmon

Ingredients:

- 4 salmon fillets
- 1/2 cup unsalted butter
- 4 cloves garlic, minced
- 1 lemon, zested and juiced
- 1 teaspoon dried dill
- Salt and black pepper, to taste
- Fresh parsley, chopped (for garnish)
- Lemon slices (for serving)

Instructions:

Pat the salmon fillets dry with a paper towel and season with salt and black pepper.
In a large skillet or shallow pan, melt the butter over medium heat.
Add minced garlic to the melted butter and sauté for 1-2 minutes until fragrant.
Place the seasoned salmon fillets into the pan, skin side down.
Pour lemon juice and sprinkle lemon zest over the salmon.
Sprinkle dried dill over the salmon for added flavor.
Cover the pan and poach the salmon in the lemon garlic butter for 8-10 minutes or until the salmon is cooked through and flakes easily with a fork.
Optional: Baste the salmon with the lemon garlic butter sauce during cooking.
Once done, carefully transfer the salmon fillets to serving plates.
Spoon the lemon garlic butter sauce over the top of each fillet.
Garnish with fresh chopped parsley.
Serve the Lemon Garlic Butter Poached Salmon with lemon slices on the side.
Enjoy this light and flavorful dish with the richness of butter, the brightness of lemon, and the savory goodness of garlic!

Honey Walnut Crusted Salmon

Ingredients:

- 4 salmon fillets
- 1/2 cup chopped walnuts
- 2 tablespoons honey
- 1 tablespoon Dijon mustard
- 1 tablespoon olive oil
- 1 teaspoon soy sauce
- Salt and black pepper, to taste
- Lemon wedges (for serving)
- Fresh parsley, chopped (for garnish)

Instructions:

Preheat the oven to 400°F (200°C).

In a bowl, mix together chopped walnuts, honey, Dijon mustard, olive oil, soy sauce, salt, and black pepper.

Pat the salmon fillets dry with a paper towel.

Place the salmon fillets on a baking sheet lined with parchment paper.

Spoon the honey walnut mixture over the top of each salmon fillet, pressing it down gently to adhere.

Bake in the preheated oven for 12-15 minutes or until the salmon is cooked through and flakes easily with a fork.

Optional: If you prefer a golden crust, broil the salmon for an additional 1-2 minutes.

Remove from the oven and let it rest for a few minutes.

Serve the Honey Walnut-Crusted Salmon with lemon wedges on the side.

Garnish with fresh chopped parsley.

Enjoy this delightful combination of sweet honey and crunchy walnuts that add a delicious crust to the salmon!

Mediterranean Salmon Salad

Ingredients:

- 4 salmon fillets
- 1 tablespoon olive oil
- 1 teaspoon dried oregano
- 1 teaspoon dried thyme
- Salt and black pepper, to taste
- 4 cups mixed salad greens
- 1 cucumber, sliced
- 1 cup cherry tomatoes, halved
- 1/2 red onion, thinly sliced
- 1/2 cup Kalamata olives, pitted
- 1/2 cup feta cheese, crumbled
- Lemon wedges (for serving)

For the Lemon Herb Vinaigrette:

- 1/4 cup olive oil
- 2 tablespoons lemon juice
- 1 teaspoon Dijon mustard
- 1 teaspoon honey
- 1 clove garlic, minced
- Salt and black pepper, to taste

Instructions:

Preheat the oven to 400°F (200°C).
Place the salmon fillets on a baking sheet lined with parchment paper.
Drizzle olive oil over the salmon fillets and sprinkle dried oregano, dried thyme, salt, and black pepper.
Bake in the preheated oven for 12-15 minutes or until the salmon is cooked through and flakes easily with a fork.
While the salmon is baking, prepare the Lemon Herb Vinaigrette by whisking together olive oil, lemon juice, Dijon mustard, honey, minced garlic, salt, and black pepper in a bowl. Set aside.

In a large salad bowl, combine mixed salad greens, sliced cucumber, cherry tomatoes, red onion, Kalamata olives, and crumbled feta cheese.

Once the salmon is done, place it on top of the salad.

Drizzle the Lemon Herb Vinaigrette over the salad and salmon.

Serve the Mediterranean Salmon Salad with lemon wedges on the side.

Enjoy this refreshing and vibrant salad that brings together the flavors of the Mediterranean with perfectly baked salmon!

Wasabi Sesame Crusted Salmon

Ingredients:

- 4 salmon fillets
- 2 tablespoons sesame seeds
- 1 tablespoon black sesame seeds (optional, for color contrast)
- 1 tablespoon wasabi paste
- 1 tablespoon soy sauce
- 1 tablespoon honey
- 1 tablespoon rice vinegar
- 1 tablespoon sesame oil
- 1 teaspoon grated ginger
- Salt and black pepper, to taste
- Green onions, sliced (for garnish)
- Sesame seeds, for garnish

Instructions:

Preheat the oven to 400°F (200°C).
In a bowl, mix together sesame seeds, black sesame seeds (if using), wasabi paste, soy sauce, honey, rice vinegar, sesame oil, grated ginger, salt, and black pepper.
Pat the salmon fillets dry with a paper towel.
Place the salmon fillets on a baking sheet lined with parchment paper.
Spoon the wasabi sesame mixture over the top of each salmon fillet, pressing it down gently to adhere.
Bake in the preheated oven for 12-15 minutes or until the salmon is cooked through and flakes easily with a fork.
Optional: If you prefer a golden crust, broil the salmon for an additional 1-2 minutes.
Remove from the oven and let it rest for a few minutes.
Garnish with sliced green onions and additional sesame seeds.
Serve the Wasabi Sesame-Crusted Salmon and enjoy the delightful combination of bold flavors!

Chimichurri Grilled Salmon

Ingredients:

- 4 salmon fillets
- Salt and black pepper, to taste

For the Chimichurri Sauce:

- 1 cup fresh parsley, finely chopped
- 1/2 cup fresh cilantro, finely chopped
- 3 cloves garlic, minced
- 1/4 cup red wine vinegar
- 1/2 cup olive oil
- 1 teaspoon dried oregano
- 1/2 teaspoon red pepper flakes (adjust to taste)
- Salt and black pepper, to taste
- Juice of 1 lime

Instructions:

Preheat the grill to medium-high heat.
Season the salmon fillets with salt and black pepper.
In a bowl, mix together chopped parsley, chopped cilantro, minced garlic, red wine vinegar, olive oil, dried oregano, red pepper flakes, salt, black pepper, and lime juice to create the chimichurri sauce.
Reserve a portion of the chimichurri sauce for serving.
Brush the grill grates with oil to prevent sticking.
Place the salmon fillets on the preheated grill and cook for 3-4 minutes per side or until the salmon is cooked through and has grill marks.
During the last minute of grilling, brush some of the chimichurri sauce over the salmon.
Remove the salmon from the grill and let it rest for a few minutes.
Serve the Chimichurri Grilled Salmon with the reserved chimichurri sauce on the side.
Enjoy this flavorful and herb-packed grilled salmon with the vibrant taste of chimichurri!

Raspberry Balsamic Glazed Salmon

Ingredients:

- 4 salmon fillets
- Salt and black pepper, to taste

For the Raspberry Balsamic Glaze:

- 1 cup fresh or frozen raspberries
- 1/4 cup balsamic vinegar
- 2 tablespoons honey
- 1 tablespoon Dijon mustard
- 1 tablespoon olive oil
- 2 cloves garlic, minced
- Salt and black pepper, to taste
- Fresh basil or mint, chopped (for garnish)

Instructions:

Preheat the oven to 400°F (200°C).
Season the salmon fillets with salt and black pepper.
In a saucepan, combine raspberries, balsamic vinegar, honey, Dijon mustard, olive oil, minced garlic, salt, and black pepper.
Bring the mixture to a simmer over medium heat, stirring occasionally. Cook for 5-7 minutes or until the raspberries break down and the sauce thickens.
Remove the sauce from heat and strain it through a fine mesh sieve to remove the raspberry seeds. Set aside.
Place the salmon fillets on a baking sheet lined with parchment paper.
Brush the salmon fillets generously with the raspberry balsamic glaze.
Bake in the preheated oven for 12-15 minutes or until the salmon is cooked through and flakes easily with a fork.
During the last few minutes of baking, brush additional glaze over the salmon.
Remove from the oven, garnish with chopped fresh basil or mint, and serve.
Enjoy this sweet and tangy Raspberry Balsamic Glazed Salmon as a delightful and colorful dish!

Tequila Lime Grilled Salmon

Ingredients:

- 4 salmon fillets
- Salt and black pepper, to taste

For the Tequila Lime Marinade:

- 1/4 cup tequila
- 1/4 cup fresh lime juice
- Zest of 1 lime
- 2 tablespoons olive oil
- 2 cloves garlic, minced
- 1 teaspoon ground cumin
- 1 teaspoon chili powder
- 1 tablespoon fresh cilantro, chopped
- Salt and black pepper, to taste

Instructions:

In a bowl, whisk together tequila, fresh lime juice, lime zest, olive oil, minced garlic, ground cumin, chili powder, chopped cilantro, salt, and black pepper to create the marinade.

Place the salmon fillets in a shallow dish and pour the tequila lime marinade over them. Make sure the salmon is well coated. Cover the dish and refrigerate for at least 30 minutes to marinate.

Preheat the grill to medium-high heat.

Remove the salmon from the marinade and let any excess marinade drip off.

Season the salmon fillets with additional salt and black pepper.

Place the salmon fillets on the preheated grill and cook for 3-4 minutes per side or until the salmon is cooked through and has grill marks.

During the last minute of grilling, brush some of the remaining marinade over the salmon.

Remove the salmon from the grill and let it rest for a few minutes.

Serve the Tequila Lime Grilled Salmon with your favorite sides.

Enjoy this zesty and flavorful grilled salmon with the bright and citrusy notes of tequila and lime!

Pistachio Crusted Salmon

Ingredients:

- 4 salmon fillets
- Salt and black pepper, to taste

For the Pistachio Crust:

- 1 cup shelled pistachios, finely chopped
- 1/4 cup breadcrumbs
- 2 tablespoons Dijon mustard
- 2 tablespoons honey
- 2 tablespoons olive oil
- 1 teaspoon lemon zest
- 1 tablespoon fresh lemon juice
- 2 tablespoons fresh parsley, chopped
- Salt and black pepper, to taste

Instructions:

Preheat the oven to 375°F (190°C).
Season the salmon fillets with salt and black pepper.
In a bowl, mix together finely chopped pistachios, breadcrumbs, Dijon mustard, honey, olive oil, lemon zest, lemon juice, chopped fresh parsley, salt, and black pepper. The mixture should have a sticky consistency.
Place the salmon fillets on a baking sheet lined with parchment paper.
Press the pistachio mixture onto the top of each salmon fillet, creating an even crust.
Bake in the preheated oven for 12-15 minutes or until the salmon is cooked through and flakes easily with a fork.
If desired, broil for an additional 1-2 minutes to crisp up the pistachio crust.
Remove from the oven and let the salmon rest for a few minutes.
Serve the Pistachio Crusted Salmon with your favorite sides.
Enjoy this elegant and nutty pistach

Mango Avocado Salmon Tartare

Ingredients:

- 8 ounces fresh salmon, finely diced
- 1 ripe mango, peeled and diced
- 1 ripe avocado, diced
- 1/4 cup red onion, finely chopped
- 1 tablespoon fresh cilantro, chopped
- 1 tablespoon fresh lime juice
- 1 tablespoon extra virgin olive oil
- Salt and black pepper, to taste
- Tortilla chips or crostini, for serving

Instructions:

In a bowl, combine the finely diced salmon, diced mango, diced avocado, chopped red onion, and chopped cilantro.
In a separate small bowl, whisk together fresh lime juice and extra virgin olive oil. Pour this dressing over the salmon mixture.
Gently toss the ingredients until well combined.
Season the tartare with salt and black pepper, adjusting to taste.
Cover the bowl and refrigerate the tartare for at least 30 minutes to allow the flavors to meld.
Just before serving, give the tartare a final gentle toss.
Spoon the Mango Avocado Salmon Tartare onto individual plates or serving dishes.
Serve with tortilla chips or crostini on the side.
Enjoy this refreshing and vibrant Mango Avocado Salmon Tartare as a delicious appetizer or light meal!

Jerk Spiced Grilled Salmon

Ingredients:

- 4 salmon fillets
- Salt and black pepper, to taste

For the Jerk Spice Rub:

- 2 teaspoons ground allspice
- 1 teaspoon dried thyme
- 1 teaspoon paprika
- 1 teaspoon onion powder
- 1 teaspoon garlic powder
- 1/2 teaspoon cayenne pepper (adjust to taste)
- 1 teaspoon brown sugar
- 1/2 teaspoon salt
- 1/2 teaspoon black pepper
- 2 tablespoons olive oil
- 2 tablespoons soy sauce
- 1 tablespoon fresh lime juice

Instructions:

Preheat the grill to medium-high heat.
In a small bowl, combine all the ingredients for the jerk spice rub: ground allspice, dried thyme, paprika, onion powder, garlic powder, cayenne pepper, brown sugar, salt, black pepper, olive oil, soy sauce, and fresh lime juice.
Season the salmon fillets with salt and black pepper.
Rub the jerk spice mixture generously over each salmon fillet, coating both sides.
Place the salmon fillets on the preheated grill and cook for 3-4 minutes per side or until the salmon is cooked through and has grill marks.
Remove the salmon from the grill and let it rest for a few minutes.
Serve the Jerk Spiced Grilled Salmon with your favorite sides.
Enjoy this flavorful and slightly spicy grilled salmon with the authentic Jamaican jerk seasoning!

Caprese Stuffed Salmon

Ingredients:

- 4 salmon fillets
- Salt and black pepper, to taste

For the Caprese Stuffing:

- 1 cup cherry tomatoes, halved
- 1 cup fresh mozzarella, diced
- 1/4 cup fresh basil, chopped
- 2 tablespoons balsamic glaze
- 2 tablespoons extra virgin olive oil
- Salt and black pepper, to taste

Instructions:

Preheat the oven to 400°F (200°C).
Season the salmon fillets with salt and black pepper.
In a bowl, combine the halved cherry tomatoes, diced fresh mozzarella, chopped fresh basil, balsamic glaze, extra virgin olive oil, salt, and black pepper. Toss until well combined.
Make a horizontal slit in each salmon fillet to create a pocket for the stuffing.
Stuff each salmon fillet with the Caprese mixture, pressing it gently into the pocket.
Place the stuffed salmon fillets on a baking sheet lined with parchment paper.
Bake in the preheated oven for 12-15 minutes or until the salmon is cooked through and flakes easily with a fork.
Remove from the oven and let the stuffed salmon rest for a few minutes.
Serve the Caprese Stuffed Salmon with additional fresh basil for garnish, if desired.
Enjoy this delightful and cheesy Caprese Stuffed Salmon for a burst of Mediterranean flavors!

Lemon Dill Salmon Burgers

Ingredients:

- 1 pound fresh salmon, skin removed, finely chopped
- 1/4 cup breadcrumbs
- 1/4 cup mayonnaise
- 1 large egg
- 2 tablespoons fresh dill, chopped
- 1 tablespoon Dijon mustard
- Zest of 1 lemon
- Salt and black pepper, to taste
- Olive oil, for cooking
- Burger buns
- Lettuce, tomato, and red onion for garnish

Instructions:

In a large bowl, combine the finely chopped fresh salmon, breadcrumbs, mayonnaise, egg, chopped fresh dill, Dijon mustard, lemon zest, salt, and black pepper. Mix until well combined.
Divide the salmon mixture into equal portions and shape them into patties.
Heat olive oil in a skillet over medium heat.
Cook the salmon burgers for 3-4 minutes per side or until they are golden brown and cooked through.
Toast the burger buns in the skillet or on a grill.
Assemble the salmon burgers by placing each patty on a bun and adding your favorite garnishes like lettuce, tomato, and red onion.
Serve the Lemon Dill Salmon Burgers with a side of your favorite sauce or additional lemon wedges.
Enjoy these flavorful and refreshing salmon burgers with a burst of lemon and dill!

Soy Ginger Glazed Salmon

Ingredients:

- 4 salmon fillets
- Salt and black pepper, to taste

For the Soy Ginger Glaze:

- 1/4 cup soy sauce
- 2 tablespoons honey
- 1 tablespoon fresh ginger, grated
- 2 cloves garlic, minced
- 1 tablespoon rice vinegar
- 1 teaspoon sesame oil
- Sesame seeds and green onions for garnish (optional)

Instructions:

Preheat the oven to 400°F (200°C).
Season the salmon fillets with salt and black pepper.
In a small saucepan, combine soy sauce, honey, grated fresh ginger, minced garlic, rice vinegar, and sesame oil. Heat the mixture over medium heat, stirring continuously, until it thickens slightly. Remove from heat.
Place the seasoned salmon fillets on a baking sheet lined with parchment paper.
Brush the soy ginger glaze over each salmon fillet, ensuring they are well-coated.
Bake in the preheated oven for 12-15 minutes or until the salmon is cooked through and flakes easily with a fork.
Remove from the oven and garnish with sesame seeds and chopped green onions, if desired.
Serve the Soy Ginger Glazed Salmon over rice or with your favorite side dishes.
Enjoy this delicious and savory salmon with a perfect balance of soy and ginger flavors!

Sweet Chili Lime Baked Salmon

Ingredients:

- 4 salmon fillets
- Salt and black pepper, to taste

For the Sweet Chili Lime Glaze:

- 1/4 cup sweet chili sauce
- Zest and juice of 2 limes
- 2 tablespoons soy sauce
- 1 tablespoon honey
- 2 cloves garlic, minced
- 1 teaspoon sesame oil
- Fresh cilantro for garnish (optional)

Instructions:

Preheat the oven to 400°F (200°C).
Season the salmon fillets with salt and black pepper.
In a bowl, whisk together sweet chili sauce, lime zest, lime juice, soy sauce, honey, minced garlic, and sesame oil to create the glaze.
Place the seasoned salmon fillets on a baking sheet lined with parchment paper.
Brush the sweet chili lime glaze over each salmon fillet, ensuring they are well-coated.
Bake in the preheated oven for 12-15 minutes or until the salmon is cooked through and flakes easily with a fork.
Remove from the oven and garnish with fresh cilantro, if desired.
Serve the Sweet Chili Lime Baked Salmon over rice or with your favorite side dishes.
Enjoy this sweet and tangy baked salmon with a burst of chili and lime flavors!

Salmon with Creamy Lemon Dill Sauce

Ingredients:

- 4 salmon fillets
- Salt and black pepper, to taste
- Olive oil for cooking

For the Creamy Lemon Dill Sauce:

- 1/2 cup plain Greek yogurt
- Zest and juice of 1 lemon
- 2 tablespoons fresh dill, chopped
- 1 tablespoon Dijon mustard
- 2 cloves garlic, minced
- Salt and black pepper, to taste

Instructions:

Season the salmon fillets with salt and black pepper.
In a bowl, mix together Greek yogurt, lemon zest, lemon juice, chopped fresh dill, Dijon mustard, minced garlic, salt, and black pepper to create the creamy lemon dill sauce.
Heat olive oil in a skillet over medium-high heat.
Cook the salmon fillets for 3-4 minutes per side or until they are golden brown and cooked through.
Remove the salmon from the skillet and set aside.
Pour the creamy lemon dill sauce into the skillet and heat it briefly, stirring to combine with any remaining salmon flavors.
Serve the salmon fillets with the creamy lemon dill sauce drizzled over the top.
Garnish with additional fresh dill if desired.
Enjoy this delightful salmon dish with a rich and creamy lemon dill sauce!

Spinach and Feta Stuffed Salmon

Ingredients:

- 4 salmon fillets
- Salt and black pepper, to taste
- Olive oil for cooking

For the Spinach and Feta Stuffing:

- 2 cups fresh spinach, chopped
- 1/2 cup feta cheese, crumbled
- 1/4 cup red onion, finely chopped
- 2 cloves garlic, minced
- 1 tablespoon olive oil
- Salt and black pepper, to taste

Instructions:

Preheat the oven to 375°F (190°C).
In a skillet, heat olive oil over medium heat. Add red onion and garlic, sautéing until softened.
Add chopped spinach to the skillet and cook until wilted. Season with salt and black pepper.
Remove the skillet from heat and let the spinach mixture cool slightly.
Stir in crumbled feta cheese and mix until well combined.
Make a horizontal cut along the side of each salmon fillet to create a pocket for the stuffing.
Stuff each salmon fillet with the spinach and feta mixture, pressing gently to close the pocket.
Season the outside of the salmon fillets with salt and black pepper.
Heat olive oil in an oven-safe skillet over medium-high heat.
Place the stuffed salmon fillets in the skillet and sear for 2-3 minutes per side.
Transfer the skillet to the preheated oven and bake for 12-15 minutes or until the salmon is cooked through and flakes easily with a fork.
Remove from the oven and let it rest for a few minutes.
Serve the Spinach and Feta Stuffed Salmon with your favorite side dishes.
Enjoy this flavorful and nutritious stuffed salmon!

Garlic Butter Tuscan Salmon

Ingredients:

- 4 salmon fillets
- Salt and black pepper, to taste
- Olive oil for cooking

For the Garlic Butter Tuscan Sauce:

- 1/2 cup cherry tomatoes, halved
- 1/2 cup sun-dried tomatoes, chopped
- 4 cloves garlic, minced
- 1 cup baby spinach
- 1 cup heavy cream
- 1/2 cup grated Parmesan cheese
- 2 tablespoons unsalted butter
- 1 tablespoon fresh basil, chopped
- Salt and black pepper, to taste

Instructions:

Season the salmon fillets with salt and black pepper.
In a skillet, heat olive oil over medium-high heat.
Sear the salmon fillets for 3-4 minutes per side or until golden brown and cooked through. Remove from the skillet and set aside.
In the same skillet, add minced garlic and sauté until fragrant.
Add cherry tomatoes, sun-dried tomatoes, and baby spinach to the skillet. Cook until the spinach wilts and the tomatoes are softened.
Pour in the heavy cream and bring the mixture to a simmer.
Stir in grated Parmesan cheese and continue to simmer until the sauce thickens.
Add butter and chopped fresh basil to the sauce. Stir until the butter is melted and the sauce is well combined.
Season the sauce with salt and black pepper to taste.
Return the seared salmon fillets to the skillet, spooning the garlic butter Tuscan sauce over them.
Simmer for an additional 2-3 minutes until the salmon is heated through.
Serve the Garlic Butter Tuscan Salmon over pasta, rice, or with your preferred side dish.

Enjoy this rich and flavorful salmon dish with a delightful Tuscan-inspired sauce!

Lemon Herb Quinoa with Salmon

Ingredients:

- 4 salmon fillets
- Salt and black pepper, to taste
- Olive oil for cooking

For the Lemon Herb Quinoa:

- 1 cup quinoa, rinsed
- 2 cups vegetable or chicken broth
- Zest of 1 lemon
- Juice of 1 lemon
- 2 tablespoons fresh parsley, chopped
- 1 tablespoon fresh dill, chopped
- Salt and black pepper, to taste

Instructions:

Season the salmon fillets with salt and black pepper.
In a skillet, heat olive oil over medium-high heat.
Sear the salmon fillets for 3-4 minutes per side or until golden brown and cooked through. Remove from the skillet and set aside.
In a saucepan, combine quinoa and broth. Bring to a boil, then reduce heat, cover, and simmer for 15-20 minutes or until the quinoa is cooked and the liquid is absorbed.
Fluff the cooked quinoa with a fork and transfer it to a serving bowl.
Add lemon zest, lemon juice, chopped parsley, and chopped dill to the quinoa. Mix well.
Season the quinoa with salt and black pepper to taste.
Serve the seared salmon fillets over a bed of lemon herb quinoa.
Garnish with additional lemon zest and fresh herbs if desired.
Enjoy this nutritious and flavorful Lemon Herb Quinoa with Salmon!

Coconut Lime Salmon Skewers

Ingredients:

- 4 salmon fillets, cut into cubes
- Salt and black pepper, to taste
- Wooden skewers, soaked in water for 30 minutes

For the Coconut Lime Marinade:

- 1/2 cup coconut milk
- Zest and juice of 2 limes
- 2 tablespoons soy sauce
- 1 tablespoon honey
- 2 cloves garlic, minced
- 1 teaspoon ground ginger
- 1 tablespoon fresh cilantro, chopped

Instructions:

In a bowl, whisk together coconut milk, lime zest, lime juice, soy sauce, honey, minced garlic, ground ginger, and chopped cilantro to create the marinade.
Season the salmon cubes with salt and black pepper.
Place the salmon cubes in a shallow dish and pour the coconut lime marinade over them. Toss to coat the salmon evenly. Cover and refrigerate for at least 30 minutes to marinate.
Preheat a grill or grill pan over medium-high heat.
Thread the marinated salmon cubes onto the soaked wooden skewers.
Grill the salmon skewers for 3-4 minutes per side or until the salmon is cooked through and has grill marks.
Serve the Coconut Lime Salmon Skewers over rice, quinoa, or your favorite side dish.
Garnish with additional chopped cilantro and lime wedges if desired.
Enjoy these tropical and zesty Coconut Lime Salmon Skewers for a delightful meal!

Walnut Pesto Salmon

Ingredients:

- 4 salmon fillets
- Salt and black pepper, to taste
- Olive oil for cooking

For the Walnut Pesto:

- 1 cup fresh basil leaves
- 1/2 cup walnuts
- 1/2 cup Parmesan cheese, grated
- 2 cloves garlic
- 1/2 cup extra-virgin olive oil
- Salt and black pepper, to taste
- Juice of 1 lemon

Instructions:

Preheat the oven to 400°F (200°C).
Season the salmon fillets with salt and black pepper.
In a food processor, combine fresh basil, walnuts, Parmesan cheese, and garlic. Pulse until finely chopped.
With the food processor running, slowly drizzle in the olive oil until the pesto reaches a smooth consistency.
Add salt, black pepper, and lemon juice to the pesto. Pulse to combine.
Heat olive oil in an oven-safe skillet over medium-high heat.
Sear the salmon fillets for 2-3 minutes per side or until golden brown.
Spoon a generous amount of walnut pesto over each salmon fillet.
Transfer the skillet to the preheated oven and bake for 10-12 minutes or until the salmon is cooked through.
Serve the Walnut Pesto Salmon over a bed of quinoa or your favorite grains.
Garnish with additional chopped basil and a drizzle of lemon juice if desired.
Enjoy this flavorful and nutty Walnut Pesto Salmon for a delicious and nutritious meal!

Cajun Salmon Alfredo Pasta

Ingredients:

- 8 oz fettuccine pasta
- 4 salmon fillets
- Cajun seasoning, to taste
- Salt and black pepper, to taste
- 2 tablespoons olive oil
- 3 cloves garlic, minced
- 1 cup cherry tomatoes, halved
- 1 cup heavy cream
- 1 cup Parmesan cheese, grated
- 1/2 cup sun-dried tomatoes, chopped
- 1 teaspoon dried basil
- Fresh parsley, chopped (for garnish)

Instructions:

Cook the fettuccine pasta according to package instructions. Drain and set aside.
Season the salmon fillets with Cajun seasoning, salt, and black pepper.
Heat olive oil in a large skillet over medium-high heat. Add the salmon fillets and cook for 3-4 minutes per side or until cooked through. Remove the salmon from the skillet and set aside.
In the same skillet, add minced garlic and sauté for 1-2 minutes until fragrant.
Add cherry tomatoes to the skillet and cook for 2-3 minutes until they start to soften.
Pour in the heavy cream and bring it to a simmer.
Stir in the grated Parmesan cheese, sun-dried tomatoes, and dried basil. Continue to stir until the cheese is melted and the sauce is smooth.
Flake the cooked salmon into bite-sized pieces and add it to the skillet. Stir gently to combine.
Add the cooked fettuccine pasta to the skillet and toss until the pasta is coated in the creamy Cajun salmon Alfredo sauce.
Season with additional Cajun seasoning, salt, and black pepper to taste.
Serve the Cajun Salmon Alfredo Pasta in individual plates, garnished with chopped fresh parsley.
Enjoy this indulgent and flavorful pasta dish with a Cajun twist!

Baked Salmon with Herbed Yogurt Sauce

Ingredients:

- 4 salmon fillets
- Salt and black pepper, to taste
- 2 tablespoons olive oil
- 1 teaspoon garlic powder
- 1 teaspoon dried dill
- 1 teaspoon dried oregano
- 1 cup Greek yogurt
- 2 tablespoons fresh lemon juice
- Zest of 1 lemon
- 2 tablespoons fresh parsley, chopped
- 1 tablespoon fresh chives, chopped

Instructions:

Preheat the oven to 375°F (190°C).

Place the salmon fillets on a baking sheet lined with parchment paper. Season with salt, black pepper, garlic powder, dried dill, and dried oregano. Drizzle olive oil over the fillets.

Bake the salmon in the preheated oven for 15-20 minutes or until the salmon is cooked through and flakes easily with a fork.

While the salmon is baking, prepare the herbed yogurt sauce. In a bowl, combine Greek yogurt, fresh lemon juice, lemon zest, chopped parsley, and chopped chives. Mix well until all the ingredients are incorporated.

Once the salmon is done, remove it from the oven and transfer the fillets to serving plates.

Spoon the herbed yogurt sauce over each baked salmon fillet.

Garnish with additional fresh herbs and lemon wedges if desired.

Serve the Baked Salmon with Herbed Yogurt Sauce alongside your favorite side dishes.

Enjoy this light and flavorful dish that combines the richness of baked salmon with the refreshing taste of herbed yogurt sauce!